ON FOOT
IN THE
EAST END
Volume II

A guide to three walks in the
East End of London

Written and Illustrated

by

Robert Philpotts

Blackwater Books

1995

*I would like to dedicate this book to two East Enders;
Miss Elleni May Onyett who is nearly one and
Mrs Annie Watkins who is nearly one hundred and one.*

Published by:
Blackwater Books, 45 Approach Road, London E2 9LY

Printed by:
Carnmor Print and Design, 95/97 London Road, Preston, Lancs.

ISBN 0946623 14 7

All text and illustrations © Robert Philpotts

First edition May 1992
This edition, in two volumes, March 1995

Cover illustration: On Wapping High Street.

Introduction to 1995 edition (Volume II).

On Foot in the East End, a guide to five walks in the East End of London, was first published in 1992 in a single volume. This second edition is issued in two volumes. The first volume has four of the walks from the 1992 edition. All have been revised and updated and one has been extended. This volume has three walks not featured in the 1992 edition but contains some material first published in the 1990 booklet *The Tower of London to Tobacco Dock*.

The following points may be helpful when using the guide.

Transport

The first two walks in this volume begin and end at tube (Underground) stations. The last walk begins at a tube station but ends at a Docklands Light Railway station, The Docklands Light Railway feeds into the tube network at Bank and Stratford.

Walking conditions and steps

With the exception of a short section of towpath on the Mile End to Three Mills walk, all the walks are routed over paved or gravelled surfaces. There are steps at all the tube stations but only on the Mile End to Three Mills walk are there flights of steps that really cannot be avoided without making a very substantial detour.

Maps

The maps are sketch maps only and not to scale.

Contents

Acknowledgements

In putting the guide together I have been helped by a number of people and should like to thank them all. I have frequently made enquiries of local residents and have invariably had a positive response whilst, in researching background, I have often used the Local History section of the Bancroft Road Library and have always found the staff there most helpful and able to locate what was wanted no matter how obscure. In checking the walks Ted Gardener and Catharine Gunningham were a great help. Barry Jones helped check both the walk and script and special thanks are due to him.

Robert Philpotts
March 1995

The Mile End to Three Mills Walk

Introduction

This walk will take you from Mile End Underground Station to Bromley-by-Bow Underground Station via Tower Hamlets Cemetery Park and the Northern Outfall Sewer. It will probably take about $2^1/4$ hours.

The River Lee (or Lea as it is sometimes spelt) has always been important for transporting commodities to and from London and it was on this waterway that the first river improvements in this country ever sanctioned by Parliament (in 1424) took place. The southern part of the Lee, especially where it is tidal, has long been a centre of industry and in his recent book *Stratford - A pictorial history* Steven Pewsey compared the area to Coalbrookdale in Shropshire as a cradle of the Industrial Revolution.

Today the Lee is much used for leisure purposes and over the past few years the Lee Valley Authority has done a good deal to develop the land alongside the river as a linear park.

This walk will take you across the border of the London boroughs of Tower Hamlets and Newham through an area which may seem rather remote. Many people consider the River Lee to mark the edge of the East End and, if you accept that all the channels and creeks in this area are really part of the river, then you will not set foot outside the East End. The most easterly path that you will walk along runs down the western side of the Chanelsea (sometimes spelt Channelsea) which is part of a complex of waterways known as 'the backs'.

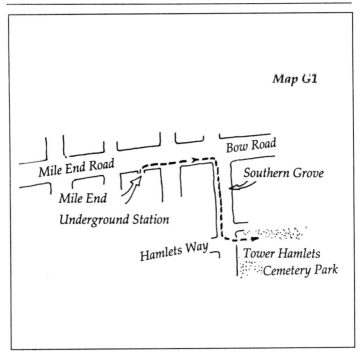

Map G1

Mile End Tube Station to Tower Hamlets Cemetery Park (Map G1)

Leave Mile End Tube Station and turn right. Now begin walking along Mile End Road. This is part of the A 11 which leads from the centre of London to south Essex. On its way it changes its name a number of times and on this walk we will know it as Mile End Road, Bow Road and Stratford High Street. Walk on over the junction with Maplin Street and then pass the *Flautist and Firkin*, a pub recently taken over and renamed by the 'real ale' Firkin Brewery. Soon you will come to the junction of Southern Grove where you should turn right and walk down until you come to the junction with Hamlets Way. Now you will see the entrance to Tower Hamlets Cemetery Park and you should go in there.

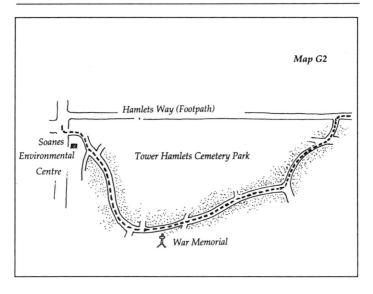

Map G2

Hamlets Way (Footpath)

Soanes
Environmental
Centre

Tower Hamlets Cemetery Park

War Memorial

Through Tower Hamlets Cemetery Park (Map G2)

Tower Hamlets Cemetery Park covers the 27 acres of the old
Tower Hamlets Cemetery which was an entrepreneurial answer
to one of the problems that faced early Victorian England. With
a rapidly rising population and full church graveyards the
question arose as to where the dead would be buried, given that
cremation was illegal. Large private graveyards seemed to
provide one answer, in the short term anyway and, in 1841, the
City of London and Tower Hamlets Cemetery Company set out
its plans for a cemetery in what was then a greenfield site. At
first everything went well but by the 1870s the area around the
cemetery had been built over as the docks brought new
industry to the area and the subsequently increased demand
for the services of the cemetery company do not seem to have
been handled well. By the 1890s the graveyard was both
overcrowded and very untidy and a 'Bow Cemetery Grievance
Committee' was pressing to get it closed - although another

seventy years were to pass before that happened.

In 1965, the cemetery (which by that time seems to have become something of an anarchical place with gangs on the roam and at least one school truant living in a tree house) was bought by the Greater London Council which then ended burials there and began to look at other uses for the land. Old graveyards in England are subject to the Disused Burial Grounds Act of 1884 which means that, with only limited exceptions, they must be left as open spaces. It would have been possible to have turned the area into one vast open field but, fortunately, local pressure managed to maintain it as a more secluded area and it is now the nearest piece of 'semi-natural' woodland to the middle of London.

Begin your walk through the park by following the path round to the right. Close to the wooden gate of the Soanes Environmental Centre you will see that the path splits and you must take the wider, left hand path flanked by large memorials and family graves. Most date from the late 19th century and show English names for the greater part, although there are some which seem to indicate a German or at least an East European origin. The gravestones seem very sombre, ivy seeks to wrap itself around them, their ornamentation is broken and weathered, the iron work rusty or wrenched away from its fitting. Those that appear to have survived best are the ones that were made of a pinkish stone with carved letters.

As the line of vaults ends you will come to a clearing where the path splits into three. Take the left path and you will come to the simple white cross of the local war memorial. After a further 40 yards or so you will see paths leading off to the left and right but you must continue straight ahead. Now you will find yourself in the middle of a well wooded area with irregular rows of headstones at the side of the path all leaning at slightly different angles. Here the ivy seems to be winning its struggle with other greenery although there are small clearings where grass seems to hold its own. Continue down the path until you come to a T-Junction. Turn left here and keep on walking until you see a gate on your left in the perimeter railings. You should leave the park through this.

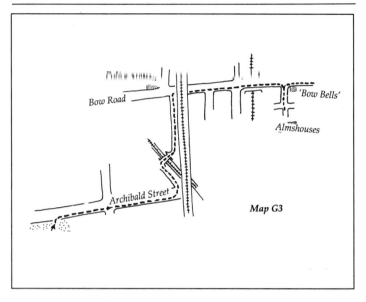

Bow Road

'Bow Bells'

Almshouses

Archibald Street

Map G3

Tower Hamlets Cemetery Park to the Bow Bells (Map G3)
On leaving the park, turn right onto the footpath and walk
along until you come to a junction with a road. This is
Wellington Way. Cross Wellington Way and walk on down
Archibald Street. At the end you will come to a railway viaduct.
Turn left here into Eleanor Street then walk a few yards along
and cross to the footbridge which leads over the railway lines.
Walk over the footbridge and at the other side turn sharp left
to walk up Arnold Road which will will take you to Bow Road.
The railway arches have all been put to good use in the usual
car tuning and panel beating way so it is a little surprising to
see, right at the end, a pink and white bar and restaurant.

Stop at the corner of Bow Road and look left and you will see
the vast facade of Thames Magistrates Court. This is the centre
of Tower Hamlets' little 'legal quarter' for, within a few hundred
yards, are a number of solicitor's offices and across the road,
housed in rather a nice building, is Bow Road Police Station.
Behind the station are stables used for police horses.

Listen for a distant whinny before turning right and walking along Bow Road. After passing under the railway bridge and crossing Tomlins Grove and Campbell Road you will soon come to Bow Church Station on the Docklands Light Railway. Walking a few yards beyond the station will bring you to the *Bow Bells* pub.

Tradition has it that no-one can call themselves a Cockney unless they were born within the sound of the Bow bells yet this poses a problem because there are two Bow churches each with their own set of bells. The one a short distance along Bow Road is St Mary's, Bow, but there is another a couple of miles away in the City of London called St Mary-le-Bow. Maybe 'within' meant 'between'. If so then both churches might claim equal rights in the tradition.

Before walking further down Bow Road it is worthwhile making a little excursion down the passage that leads between the *Bow Bells* and Marsalis House. As you pass onto the road at the other end (Rainhill Way) you will see, almost straight ahead, a terrace of red-brick almshouses. Go right up close and you will observe, above the central door, an ornate plaque indicating that this little building partly owes its existence to a 'saylemaker' named John Edmundson. Mr Edmundson must have plied his trade in the late 17th century and, though the canvas sails and the wooden ships that they powered have long since disintegrated, it is pleasing to think that the charitable use of his profits have helped provide shelter for nearly three hundred years.

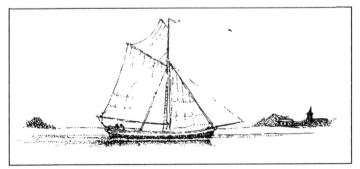

Dick Whittington

When Dick Whittington (and cat) were about to leave the outskirts of London they were called back by the sound of Bow Bells. The question of whether it was Bow Church in the city or Bow Church near the Lee has never been settled but supporters of the eastern Bow say the sound of their bells would have rung out clearly over the fields towards Highgate. Perhaps a dusty manuscript in Dick's own hand lies in a vault somewhere and, when discovered, will clear the matter up for good.

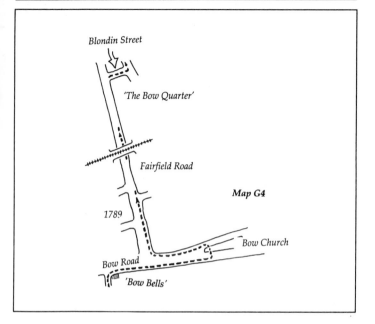

Map G4

The Bow Bells to Blondin Street (Map G4)

Return to the *Bow Bells* and turn right. After about 30 yards you will come to Bromley Public Hall which now houses the Tower Hamlets Register Office and where you might very occasionally see a few tiny coloured paper horseshoes on the pavement. Confetti must be one of the least offensive forms of litter and the people who throw it often tuck the boxes behind the metal bars that stand on either side of the steps. I always thought that these were boot scrapers but maybe they are confetti-box holders craftily designed to blend into the old facade.

Leaving Bromley Public Hall, walk about 150 yards to a pedestrian crossing which will take you to an island which divides Bow Road. Cross to the island and you will find yourself at a statue of the Victorian prime minister, W. E. Gladstone,

The statue once stood in the grounds of the nearby Bryant and May match factory. On the plinth, you will see an indication that it was a gift from one of the Bryant family but this is hardly the whole truth for the poorly paid workers at the factory had money deducted from their wages to help pay for it. Resentful of their enforced contributions, some of the aggrieved workers ('matchgirls' as they were called) made their way to the unveiling ceremony armed with stones and bits of brick. In the melee that followed, some workers evidently cut their arms to let the blood trickle onto the marble, for, as the social reformer Annie Besant said, it had been *'paid for, in very truth, by their blood.'*

W.E. Gladstone

William Ewart Gladstone's favourite exercise was energetically cutting wood. Fittingly, an anagram of his name is 'A wild man will go at trees'.

Right behind the statue a footpath runs down to St Mary's Church. In the early 12th century, local people complained that the winter floods made it impossible for them to get to their regular place of worship and so a 'Chapel of Ease' was built for them on this spot. About two hundred years later this was converted to a full parish church and that building, set within its coffin shaped grounds, has been a landmark for centuries for travellers between London and Essex. It has not always been a welcome sight, however, because before there were clear regulations as to which side of the church respective flows of traffic should pass, those in charge of carts and coaches tended to take pot luck. As a result, there were frequent traffic jams and occasionally calls that the church be moved. At the time of the reign of Queen Anne it seems that land was bought nearby so that a new church could be built but local residents, anxious that they would have to pay a tax to fund it, offered to build a new house on the ground for the minister. He agreed evidently and so the old church remained where it was and congestion continued. A journal published in the late 18th century ran a series of items about metropolitan annoyances and focused on the congestion at Bow. *'The nuisance,'* it complained, *'continues and is likely to continue for half a century longer'* - yet a century later debate was still taking place about traffic problems with any suggestion of demolition likely to stir up a first class row.

In the end the demolishers never did get their way, even though a 1941 bomb did a good deal of work for them and, today, the church still maintains its position in the middle of the highway. Strangely, those in the traffic which now passes by its sides often find the road here to be less congested than that either to the east or west so perhaps building churches in the middle of roads is one answer to our traffic problems!

Leave the island by the pedestrian crossing so that you cross Bow Road completely. Now turn left and begin walking towards Fairfield Road. You will pass the *The Kings Arms* pub and then come to a launderette, one of those (mostly) unsung institutions which make the wheels of life go just that bit more smoothly. A couple of doors beyond the launderette is a

building that dates from the time of wash tubs and mangles. Look up and you will see the date 1919 and a rare example of a beehive, an old Co-operative Society 'logo'. Note that the plaque was erected by the Stratford Co-op which was a large local organisation of the time and which, after its amalgamation with the Edmonton Society in 1920, formed the basis of the London Co-op of today. Control of this organisation was the subject of political struggle in the early years of this century with the more liberal 'founding' elements being challenged by a new group of socialists. Alfred Barnes was one of the left-wingers and he won the crucial post of President in 1915. Although he lost the position in 1918, he regained it in 1919 and it is his name which you can see beneath the bees. Barnes went on to become the Labour and Co-operative Member of Parliament for East Ham and eventually served as a minister in Clem Attlee's post Second World War Labour Government.

A few yards from the old co-op is the junction of Fairfield Road and Bow Road. Right on the opposite corner you will see Bow House.

Bow House was originally built as a town hall for the old Borough of Poplar and, when under construction, was regarded as being the first town hall in the country to be built in the 'modern' style. It was, in a way, a symbol of forward thinking local authority endeavour for, in the inter-war period, Poplar was known nationwide for its radical approach to social problems connected with poverty and to the financing of services designed to deal with them. One of the leading figures of this movement (which took the name 'Poplarism') was George Lansbury who went on to be the leader of the Labour Party and it was fitting that he should have been the man invited to open the hall when it was completed in December 1938.

Vision had certainly been shown in its design and on the day when the foundation stone had been laid, the architect made a speech which showed he had a far from detached and apolitical approach to his task. He said:

'Whilst my son and myself as architects to this building are proud to be entrusted with this work, we, with those who are gathered here, trust that the new kingdom of righteousness which you are seeking to establish may also have had its foundation stone well and truly laid by the works of yourself and other pioneers in the cause of humanity'

An architect is one of the five figures shown in bas-relief on the corner of the building and, like the other four (representing a labourer, a stone-mason, a carpenter and an acetylene welder), was carved after the sculptor had made on-site sketches when construction was taking place.

Poplar Town Hall was intended to be more than just an

administrative centre, those involved in the project seeking to make a continental style civic centre, something like the town

hall of Copenhagen which was a 'people's palace' and in consequence a large theatre-cum-dancehall was featured in the design. This was not long in being put to use. On the evening of the opening, half-a-crown (12 $^1/_2$p) tickets ensured entrance to a dance featuring the music of Stan Bloomfield and his Harlem Band.

In the 1960s, Poplar was absorbed into the London Borough of Tower Hamlets and so lost a need for a town hall. The theatre continued to operate in municipal hands until the late 80s and, amongst others, Gene Pitney, the Stylistics and Hale and Pace played there but audience figures were not high enough to maintain it as a major venue. Today, renamed as Bow Hall, it serves as offices.

Turn down Fairfield Road. After a few yards you will come to the junction of Paton Close and on the corner you will see a little restaurant called the *1789*. The unusual name takes its inspiration from the year of the revolution that turned France downside up. The restaurant is, naturally, French. On several occasions I have looked closely at the menu to see if there were any evocative dishes but have only ever found Fillet Napoleon. There are, however, Legumes d'Amour - and it's better to make L'Amour than La Guerre I suppose. Try *1789*, it is very good.

Continue on down Fairfield Road and you will pass the junction of Wrexham Road and the Bow bus garage. Given the great changes that have taken place in bus services since deregulation we should, I think, look on this garage as a kind of sanctuary. Look through the doors and you might see the buses standing quietly and having their red skins polished before going off to slurp diesel. Every so often one will appear around the corner with its handler ready to trundle off up to Victoria or Oxford Circus. In 1994 there were distant Euro-rumbles that, some said, could lead to the extinction of the double decker bus so, surely, the time has come to make these tame and friendly vehicles a protected species.

Continue down Fairfield Road and go under the railway bridges and you will come to a vast complex of red brick buildings. This is the old Bryant and May match factory where the statue of Gladstone once stood.

The works were opened in the 1860s and, despite the well known danger of sickness from handling the phosphorous which was used in match production, the company had no

trouble in recruiting labour. Conditions were harsh and though the pay was low there were fines and stoppages for even minor transgressions. It was here, in the early 1880s that the incident around Gladstone's statue took place and, by the end of that decade, things were reaching boiling point. In June of 1888, Annie Besant published *White Slavery in London* which exposed the poor conditions and petty tyranny which was the order of the day in the Fairfield works and began to distribute it outside the factory gates. The management responded by sacking three girls whom they suspected of feeding Besant information but this led to a mass walkout. At first the company treated their employees' actions with some contempt, believing that lack of money would soon force them back to work but the plight of the girls was well publicised and it soon became a cause celebre. Money began to come from all over the country to help them and, as the girls began to organise themselves into a union, the call went out for a boycott of Bryant and May matches. As a result of all this pressure the employers were forced into a humiliating climbdown and the 'matchgirls' were able to return to work under a less strict regime and better general conditions. It was a significant victory for 'non-craft' industrial workers who previously had been without the muscle of unionisation and, particularly, for exploited female labour.

Bryant and May continued to make matches at the factory until around twenty five years ago but today the old factory has been given a radically new lease of life as a huge complex of apartments. These are advertised with an American flavour and, if you peer through the gates, you will see that the access roads have New York-ish names.

Continue up Fairfield Road to Blondin Street on the right.

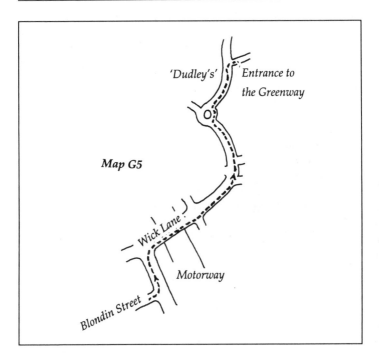

Blondin Street to the Greenway (Map G5)
Turn down Blondin Street and walk right to the end and you
will come to a blue plaque which indicates that the Clayhall Tea
House once stood there. Rather than being just a tea house,
however, it seems as though the Clay Hall was something of an
18th century 'leisure complex'. Tea was served for sure but
stronger stuff could be had at a nearby tavern. There was also
a little tree covered knoll - for gentle perambulation presumably
- and a model mill. This mill is intriguing for tradition had it
that it could grind up old folks and make them young again. No
sign of the complex remains today and, more importantly, no
sign of the mill either. Imagine what you could charge to use
it if you found it! Think of the queues!

Exit from Blondin Street and turn left into Wick Lane. After walking a few yards you will come to a busy spot where the traffic exits from the road below. Turn right here and walk over the bridge. Look right and you will see, in the distance, Bow flyover which takes traffic over ground which was once tricky for travellers. One story has it that Queen Matilda of Scotland, spouse of Henry I, got a washing in the River Lee as she negotiated a ford hereabouts and, in consequence, had a bridge built to save others from the same fate. Because the bridge was arched like a bow, it was called Bow Bridge. That's one story anyway. It certainly is true that this area has often been difficult for those making the journey between London and places beyond Stratford, primarily because the River Lee splits itself into several channels. Collectively, these channels are known as the Bow Backs and we will keep coming across them as we continue our walk.

Keep on walking down Wick Lane and you will eventually come to a roundabout. Turn right at the roundabout and walk along, passing the Dudley stationery company on the left. The road rises to cross the Northern Outfall Sewer and, just before the brow of the hump, you will see a large sign on the right indicating the start of a path called the Greenway. Access to the Greenway is through the combined pedestrian, cycle and pram gates and you should pass through these on to the footpath beyond.

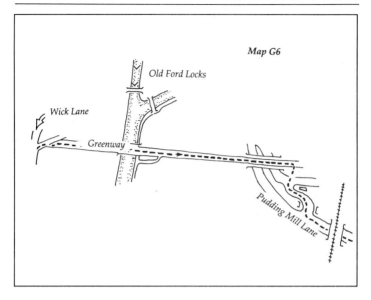

Map G6

Old Ford Locks

Wick Lane

Greenway

Pudding Mill Lane

Along the Greenway; Wick Lane to Pudding Mill Lane (Map G6)

The Northern Outfall Sewer on which the Greenway runs was a marvel of mid-Victorian civil engineering. Sewage removal was a perennial problem for London and tackled in a piecemeal way which was never satisfactory in the long term. By the 1840s, matters were reaching something of a crisis point. There were thousands of miles of sewers but they emptied into the Thames at various points and turned the river into a foul smelling waterway very conducive to the spread of disease. In 1847, an Act of Parliament forced the destruction of more than two hundred thousand London cesspits and obliged property owners to connect to the sewers. However, this made the Thames even more polluted and, in the 1850s, after real fears of a widespread epidemic caused by the effluent in the Thames, it was decided to build a great new system of tunnels and pipes south and north of the Thames which would dump the sewage miles from the centre of the city. Several designs were put forward and one by an engineer named Joseph Bazalgette was accepted. North of the river, Mr Bazalgette envisaged three lines of sewers which would meet in east London. The high level sewer would run from Hampstead, the middle level from Kensal Green (via Oxford Street and the City) and the Lower level from Chelsea. After converging, the sewage would run down to an outflow at Barking Creek 14 miles below London Bridge and, released at high water, would then be carried down towards the sea as the tide ebbed.

A couple of hundred yards from the entrance to the Greenway, you will come to a bridge which crosses the River Lee. It is a wide bridge and is really a cover for the great pipes which run underneath. Stop here for a moment and take in the view.

More than a thousand years ago, this river was part of a boundary that ran from the Thames to the Mersey. To the west was the land of the Saxons, to the east the area controlled by invading Danes. At one time it had seemed that the whole country might be overrun by the fierce men who crossed the North Sea in their shallow draught boats (all the better to get up rivers like the one below) and fall on the little settlements of ill-prepared Saxon farmers. In the nick of time a young Saxon king, Alfred, emerged and gave the Danes a sharp reverse. After the Battle of Edington in 878, the country was divided in two - so crossing this area means you are crossing from the land of one ancient kingdom to another. Legend has it that the backs themselves may have been created on Alfred's command in order to split the flow of the Lee and so make the water of the various channels so shallow that the Danish boats would be trapped.

Before you go over the bridge you will see a squat, six-sided building and four obstructive concrete posts. A little over a thousand years after Alfred's reign the Lee was the scene of defence works again. This time the potential invaders were under the control of Hitler's generals and the British military planners of half a century ago soon saw what a vital point this bridge was. Possession of it not only allowed domination of the river below but also allowed access to either bank and the land beyond. In the event the invasion never came and, though

German soldiers did end up in Victoria Park, they were in a prisoner of war compound. One would imagine that nothing would remain of their presence today and yet, in the early 80s, I was in the park and saw someone find a German coin dating from the early 1940s, presumably dropped by a POW.

If you are startled by a crash, bang and wallop whilst looking at the pill-box don't fear that a long delayed bomb fuse has detonated - the source will probably be the garden of the old lock cottages that can be seen over the left bridge parapet. Why? Look closely in the back garden and you will see a huge dish pointing skywards. At dawn, the cottages turn into a TV studio from where the zany Channel 4 'Big Breakfast' is broadcast.

Looking over the other side of the bridge you will see several factories. In the 19th century, closeness to London and good water communications by river and canal made the Lee an attractive place to manufacturers but, even before that, there were thriving industrial concerns. The most famous was the Bow China factory which was established on the banks of the river in the 1730s. At that time a good deal of porcelain was being imported and two compelling arguments for the establishment of the works were that *'it would not only save large sums of money that were paid yearly to the Chinese and Saxons but also employ large numbers of men, women and children'* (by this time 'Saxons' meant Germans rather than the followers of Alfred!). The factory was evidently modelled on one in Canton, China and so took the name *New Canton.* How much money *New Canton* eventually diverted from importers is unknown but it certainly provided work and at its peak employed about 600 people, attracting skilled artisans with adverts like one which read *'painters in blue and white and enamellers on china and a person who can model small figures in clay neatly, would meet with employment and proper encouragement according to their merit, by applying at the counting-house at the China-house near Bow'.* The factory seems to have thrived for about 40 years and its wares were displayed and sold through a showroom in Cornhill. Then, in 1775, the whole works was sold to a man who wanted to re-establish it elsewhere. It must have been rather sad for those who had grown up near what was really quite a famous factory to see the whole place being emptied lock, stock and barrel, but off everything went to a new home in the Midlands. I wonder if any Derby folk can trace their ancestry to potters who learnt their skills in Bow and then were offered a chance to keep their employment if they would move?

Walk on across the bridge and continue straight down the pebbled path. In summer this is a good spot to do a little blackberry picking. Walk right along the path and you will soon pass a last resting place of yesterday's motoring joys, where family saloons of a decade ago (look at the number plates - scrap yards are now seeing the alphabet start all over again) are cannabalised to keep their contemporaries going for another couple of MOTs. A few yards further on you will come to another bridge with black and white pebbles placed in such a way as to represent the logo of Thames Water. Below this bridge, visible from the road which runs beneath it, is a curious plate which indicates that this is the site of the ancient river wall and that it is the job of the landowner to keep the ground level to a certain height - presumably to avoid flooding. That height is marked but it is now some ten feet above the ground!

Beyond the bridge, the path is eventually cut by a railway line and so you must turn right immediately after the bridge and make your way down the steps to the road below. At the bottom of the steps you must cross Marshgate Lane and walk up the incline which leads to an old brick bridge. Cross the bridge, which now spans only weeds and grass, and then turn left at the junction with Pudding Mill Lane. Walk along Pudding Mill Lane and you will pass under bridges which carry the railway. Note as you go the way in which the edge of the brick span has had to be repaired and the scrape marks which indicate years of misjudgement by unfortunate drivers. The last little bridge you come to serves the Docklands Light Railway.

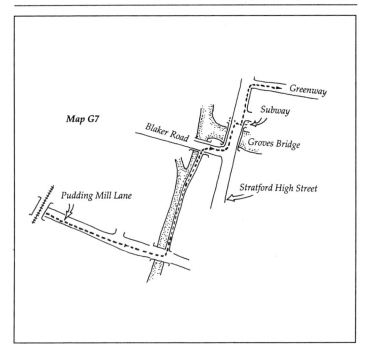

Map G7

Greenway

Subway

Groves Bridge

Blaker Road

Stratford High Street

Pudding Mill Lane

Pudding Mill Lane to the eastern part of the Greenway (Map G7)

Few would consider the next section of this walk to be very inspiring and, to pass the time, you might be tempted to sing a little song or, alternatively, you might just like to hum. But if you can't even be bothered to do that then London Electricity has thoughtfully provided a humming station on the right, a couple of hundred yards beyond the bridge.

A few yards beyond the electricity station you will come to a bridge. The big building beyond the bridge on the right is built on the spot where one of the factories of the old Bow China factory stood but there is nothing to be seen of that now. You must leave the bridge by the towpath which you will see leading down to the left. Walk along the pebbled towpath and you will shortly come to a junction of waterways with a set of defunct locks. The lock keeper's cottage stands a few yards away where, since there is no need to keep a lookout for passing boats anymore, the garden is pleasantly overgrown.

Continue along the towpath and you will have to walk up a ramp which will bring you on to another bridge. This carries the short Blaker Road. Today, most people who come to this road are probably not in the best of temper. Some are angry, some frustrated; all will be lighter in the purse or wallet department for Blaker Road is where illegally parked cars are taken to when they are hauled away by the Removal Units. When researching this walk I had a look through the wire that guards the compound. There, right in the middle was an ice cream van and

I had a sudden vision of someone of tender years waiting patiently by the window listening for a few bars of the *Harry Lime Theme* or *Colonel Bogey* as, round the corner, the van was being whisked away on the back of a truck with chequered blue tape down the side. Sentimental tosh of course - it was probably fleecing the tourists on quadruple yellow lines and causing a grid lock from Dulwich to Dollis Hill.

Before you leave Blaker Road, stand by the eastern parapet of the bridge and look over the side in the opposite direction to the lock keepers cottage. Straight ahead, an aqueduct carries Mr Bazalgette's pipes and behind that you will see an incongruous painting of flower sellers on the wall of a building once occupied by Yardley's, a company that always specialised in scented toiletries. I have been told that, by lunchtime, sandwiches brought by shopfloor employees were likely to have absorbed a perfume. I wonder what potted meat and Lavender tasted like?

Leave Blaker Road by turning right and walking to the main road, a continuation of Bow Road which has now become Stratford High Street. Turn left here and walk over the bridge. This is Groves Bridge which was constructed in the early 1930s as part of a general flood prevention programme in the area. This must have provided a different kind of relief to many people too, given the fact that the project was undertaken in the worst years of the Depression. Once over the bridge, which has the rubble of previous bridges in the foundations of its approaches, you will see a sign to a subway which you should take to get to the other side of the road. Once there, continue to walk away from the bridge down Stratford High Street. After crossing Abbey Lane you will shortly come to the entrance to the eastern part of the Greenway on the right and you should walk on to it.

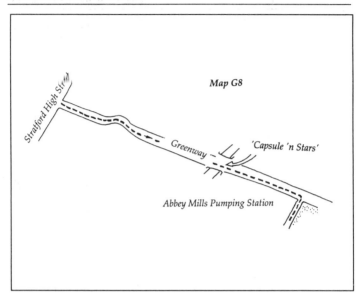

Stratford High Street to the Chanelsea River (Map G8)

The Greenway runs on for some distance from here and is a delightful high level path. Our walk only goes along it for a short way but you might consider exploring it all on some other day. For the present, walk along until you come to the Abbey Mills Bridge and then try and make out what the 'pebble mosaic' there may represent. Stumped? So was I until I read on the nearby signboard that the Greenwich Meridian line runs right over the bridge. The line of pebbles traces the Meridian line and the capsule, moon and stars the 1969 Apollo landing. I wonder how many other towns and cities in the world mark the Meridian line. There is a marker at Waltham Abbey, I know, but what about all the other thousands of places that it must pass over? Time for a club, surely - or Meridian Twinning.

Continue along the Greenway and almost straight away you will be able to get a good view of the Abbey Mills Pumping Station.

The Abbey Mills Pumping Station was an integral part of the sewage disposal plan put forward by Mr Bazalgette. Its purpose was to pump waste up from the lowest sewer so that it could continue its journey to Barking under the force of gravity. If constructed today the station would probably be a slab sided building, concrete and utilitarian but, as you can see, the temper of Mr Bazalgette's times was different. Those responsible for water supply often do a good job in preserving their Victorian heritage and the main building is a tribute to more than one and a quarter centuries of careful maintenance. The cruciform plan of the station allowed four pairs of engines to be set facing a central point and, when operating, these drove the sewage pumps. The eight 142 hp expansive, condensive, rotative beam engines gave good service until they were replaced in the 1930s.

Originally, two tall tapering chimneys stood between the bank of the sewer and the station (you may still see their bases) but these were knocked down during the Second World War as it was believed that enemy pilots were using them as markers when attempting to bomb local gasometers.

Bazalgette's sewage system must be in the first rank of those 19th century civil engineering projects which improved life for Victorian Londoners and he was granted a knighthood in 1874. Yet there were some people who considered that they had had their health hazards worsened by the north bank sewer for, in 1869, a petition was presented to the House of

Commons by citizens of Barking, the place where the contents of the Outfall finally fell out. They complained that they were having to put up with *'the filth and refuse of the largest city in the world in all its horrors and abominations'*. Evidently there were banks of solid sewage 8 or 9 feet deep on the riverbank and Barking Creek seems sometimes to have been in a terrible state because of untreated, floating effluent. This situation was not properly resolved until the construction of the Beckton Sewage Works some years later.

You must now walk along to the steps which you will see a short distance away where a signpost points to Three Mills. Before you leave the Greenway, look at the little signboard that stands nearby and then go up the steps and stand at the top for a moment. You may see a tube train clatter by a few hundred yards away. Hidden behind the office block is West Ham Underground Station (although it is above ground) for you are now several hundred yards outside the London Borough of Tower Hamlets. Go east, beyond West Ham, and you will find East Ham. Both of these places now lie in a borough which, inevitably, is called Newham. This borough now advertises itself as the 'Heart of East London' yet West Ham maintained its sturdy independence for most of its life and, indeed, this was one reason for the expansion of the area in the 19th century. Along with cheap land and a good water supply, a relatively light local authority hand lay upon industrial concerns and this attracted investment. In 1910 the West Ham Borough Council published a leaflet entitled *West Ham, the factory centre of the South of England*. According to a survey conducted in 1907, the largest group of firms at that time were those involved in chemicals and this industry had strong links with Germany. I wonder if any of the families whose memorials stand in Tower Hamlets Cemetery Park came to the east side of London on the promise of prosperity in West Ham?

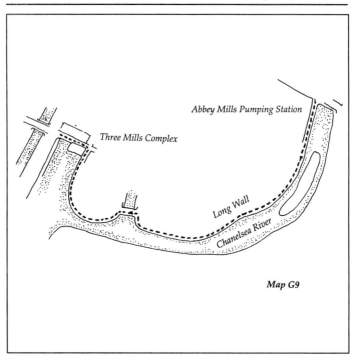

Abbey Mills Pumping Station

Three Mills Complex

Long Wall

Chanelsea River

Map G9

The Greenway to Three Mills (Map G9)

Going down the steps will put you on a path which will take you alongside the Chanelsea River (sometimes called Abbey Creek just here). The path is called the Long Wall and has recently been upgraded. Though the signs of modern life never fully disappear from view, it is less difficult here to imagine what life was like when West Ham was more famous for corn than for chemicals. For nearly half of the last 800 years the area was dominated by the Abbey of Stratford Longthorne which lay close by and which must have made a substantial part of its wealth from harnessing water power to grinding wheels. Founded in 1135, the Cistercian Abbey lasted for a few years longer than four centuries. It was swept away by the Dissolution of the 1530s but, monastic house or no monastic house, the bakers still needed flour and the mills that the abbey had owned were straightaway grinding for new proprietors.

Eventually the path will bring you out at a bridge which will take you over a flood channel and then, after you pass a 'designer graffitied' wall the Three Mills complex will come into view. These mills were originally owned by Stratford Abbey although, of course, the structures you see are the results of building work done long after the death of Henry VIII. Nonetheless, there is a continuous link that runs back from the present to the time of the Domesday Book when eight mills were reported as being in West Ham - all, probably, being water mills on the Lee. Almost certainly few visitors to the mills have been less welcome than those Domesday snoopers who arrived in the 1080s. It must have been obvious that the results of their careful, quill penned record keeping would only be more taxation. And how would the tax be raised? Harder work from those employed by the grinding wheels, of course.

At the end of the riverside walk you will come out on to a road. Turn left. After a few yards you will see a visitor's centre in a new building which stands on the site of the old millers house (demolished after the Second World war because of bomb damage). Next door to the centre is the House Mill and opposite the Clock Mill.

Though nothing is ground at the House Mill today, a new chapter in its life is being written by the River Lee Tidal Mill Trust. The trust is gradually renovating the mill, the largest and most powerful of its type in the country. Within the massive timber frame of this mill four water wheels were installed which, when working together, could generate almost as much power as one of the original steam engines that drove the pumps at Abbey Mills Pumping Station. They were turned by harnessing the power of the sea - or rather storing the power of the sea and releasing it over several hours. As the tide comes in so it turns the flow of the Thames and its tributaries the 'wrong' way and the water level of the rivers rise. At Three Mills, when the tide was at its highest point, there was a potential 'mill pond' to the rear of the House Mill covering more than 50 acres and stretching for about three miles right up to Lee Bridge. As the tide went out so this water was trapped and then gradually released to drive the wheels by an 'undershot' process. The turning water wheels drove the grinding wheels which did the actual work of the mill, turning grain into flour or meal. This was then put into bags to be transported to its destination by barge or waggon.

Working in the mills was never an easy job, the banging and clattering, the heavy sacks, the fine dust and the interminably revolving wheels giving little respite from the arduous labour needed to produce flour yet the work was offered, and taken, for century after century until new forms of power made this type of mill uneconomic. I suppose working in a tidal mill had certain benefits denied to those who toiled in windmills. At least there was a rhythm here dictated by the forces of the oceans whilst, in a windmill, several still days must have been followed by panic stations and endless hours of work as the windmiller tried to reduce the backlog of work.

As time goes by there are plans to develop the whole of the area surrounding the House Mill more fully. There is already a workshop where the renovation of fairground equipment takes place and it is possible that this may be complemented by a museum. Open ground close by will be landscaped to improve its amenity value. All in all the future looks much more rosy now than it did twenty five years ago when it seemed as though the Three Mills Complex would end up in the hands of a demolition company.

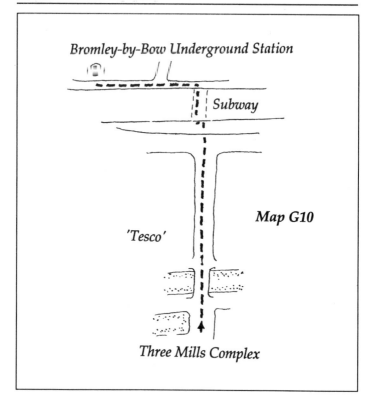

The Three Mills to Bromley-by-Bow (Map G10)

This is effectively the end of our walk and all that remains to do now is to walk to the tube station. Leave Three Mills and walk over the bridge and past the Tesco Supermarket. A little beyond that is the busy main road and you should go to the other side by the subway. Exit from the subway by the steps on the left and then walk along the roadside pavement, cross St Leonards Road and you will come to Bromley-by-Bow Station.

The Tower of London to Tobacco Dock Walk

Introduction

This walk will take you from Tower Hill Underground Station to Wapping Underground Station. It should take about 1 ¹/₄ hours. It may also be used as the first part of a walk between the Tower of London and Canary Wharf.

The use of London's riverfront has always been something of a barometer of the changing economic climate in which the city has existed. In Roman times merchants brought all kinds of goods to the wharves but, as the Empire began to collapse, a long period of decline began which may have resulted in the virtual cessation of trading activity. Not until the establishment of fairly stable Saxon kingdoms in the 7th century did the fortunes of London revive but then began a continuous period of development which has lasted until the present day.

Security has always been vital for trade and the buildings at either end of this walk were constructed with this in mind. Initially the Tower of London, which was begun in the 11th century, must have seemed very intimidatory to those who made their living on and by the river - but it also offered a measure of security from an attack from the east. On the other hand the Tobacco Dock buildings were originally part of a complex constructed to guard against opportunistic theft from from insecure warehouses and ships moored in the River Thames which, by the 18th century, had become very overcrowded.

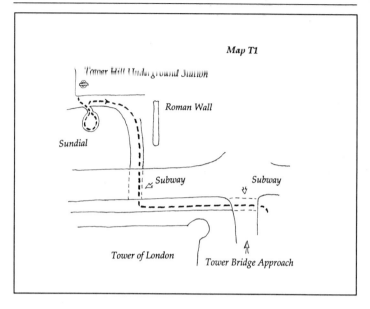

Map T1

Tower Hill Underground Station

Roman Wall

Sundial

Subway   *Subway*

Tower of London

Tower Bridge Approach

Tower Hill Underground to Tower Bridge Approach (Map T1)

Leave Tower Hill Underground Station and you will see a little observation platform up a ramp. Walk up the ramp and you will find a giant sundial on which the history of London is set out in relief. Nearby is a metal plate which indicates buildings in the area, the main focus being, of course, the Tower of London.

The Tower of London was begun by William the Conqueror, that energetic, ruthless and lucky king who first seized power from the English Harold and then imposed his Norman will through a massive programme of castle building. The White Tower, which is the central building of the present Tower of London, was partly constructed of limestone imported from France and, dominating the old Saxon town, immediately became a symbol of a new era, part garrison barracks and part protective fortress.

Nine centuries have brought many changes but the Tower still has an important security function, one of which is to prevent a repetition of events in 1671 when Captain Blood attempted to run off with the Crown Jewels. It remains a royal palace and, in an emergency, it can serve as a secure prison. Rudolf Hess, the deputy of Adolf Hitler, was incarcerated here after landing in Scotland in an eccentric, single handed attempt to bring an end to the Second World War.

William the Conqueror was not the first man to see the advantages of this position in defending a sizeable settlement. Look to the left of the observation circle and you will see a wall that, though much repaired and added to, dates from nearly 2000 years ago when the Romans created Londinium, first as a military base and then as the capital city of their province of Britannia.

Make your way towards the Roman wall by going back down to the station exit then turning right. Walk along and, bearing right, go down the steps to the patch of grass which lies before the wall. A statue of the Roman Emperor Trajan stands here and, close by, is a large plaque which replicates one found in a nearby graveyard. The original stood over the body of Gaius

45

Julius Alpinus Classicianus, a man who must have played an important part in the first turbulent years of the Roman occupation. Like many conquerors the Romans had to deal with the odd rebellion. The most serious was led by Queen Boadacea who by all (Roman) accounts seems to have been a woman of striking appearance and substantial will. She attacked the new town, set fire to it and massacred the inhabitants but

Boadacea

She was very tall and looked terrifying with a fierce glint in her eye and a harsh voice.... A great mass of hair hung to her hips.

Roman description

was then defeated by the disciplined veterans of the 14th Legion. Unwilling to face the humiliation of being a prisoner in Roman hands she poisoned herself leaving her people, the Iceni, to face the wrath of the victors. Fortunately for the peace of the province wise counsel prevailed in Rome and pacifying, rather than vindictive officials were given power in the post-rebellion period. Classicianus was one of these.

Leaving the Roman relics, go down the steps and through the tunnel towards the Tower and, on reaching the edge of the dried up moat, turn left towards St. Katharine Dock. A hundred yards or so along you will go through another tunnel under Tower Bridge Approach.

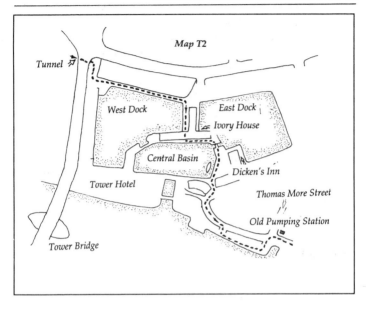

Map T2

Tower Bridge Approach to Thomas More Street (Map T2)
Close by the exit from the tunnel you will see a little footbridge
bearing a path that goes off to the right. Cross it, walk through
the small garden that has echoes of Japan and round the left
hand corner by the stones that mark the position of the Roman
amphitheatre. You will now see St Katharine Dock before you.

This dock was one of a series built in the early 19th century
when Britain was an expanding industrial power. London had
an important role to play in this time of rapid economic growth
and good facilities were a key factor in the efficient movement
of commodities. The capital had, of course, always been
important as a port but, by the late 18th century, the river
trade was suffering from an antiquated system of processing
goods through customs, chronic overcrowding on the water
and increasing robbery from vulnerable vessels and wharfs.
The obvious solution was to build docks surrounded by high

walls so that ships could get off the river and unload their cargoes free from the threat of theft.

Thomas Telford was the engineer responsible for the building of St Katharine Dock, a man who, at the end of a lifetime of road, bridge and canal building oversaw the construction of a compact dock in which hardly a square yard of ground was wasted. A good deal of demolition had to take place before building began, of course, and one venerable institution which had to move was based on the medieval church of St Katharine-by-the-Tower. As compensation, a collegiate church of St Katharine was built miles away in Regents Park. Eventually, after more than a century, the Royal Foundation of St Katharine made its way back east and you will pass its modern home if you do the third walk in this volume.

Where the old church and associated hospital once stood there are now three irregularly shaped basins and the first you will see is a kind of rest home for ageing barges, craft which have earned a living in the creeks and inlets of the south and

east coasts. Walk along the north side of the pool (called the West Dock) and then turn right but give a left handed glance to the model elephants which stand guard over the dock gates. I do not know if any elephants were ever landed at the dock but their tusks certainly were and so were those of pre-historic mammoths dug up from the frozen ground of Siberia. The Ivory House takes its name from this trade. Originally built in 1854 as 'I' warehouse by Aitcheson Senior, it fell into dereliction after the closure of the docks in 1968 but was converted and renovated in the early 1970s as the centrepiece of the new complex. It now houses shops, apartments and offices and old vaults have been changed into a banqueting hall.

Look along the side of the West Dock and you will see your way through Ivory House to the Central Basin. When you get to the Central Basin stop for a moment and take in the view. Almost directly ahead is the red steel framework of the bridge which spans the entrance to the dock. The raising of the bridges (there is a second, wooden structure closer to the

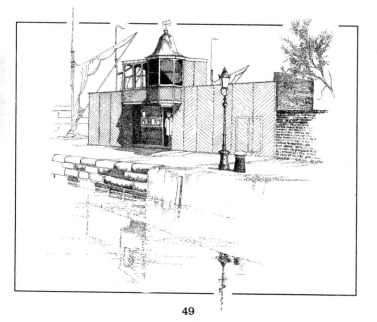

Thames) is controlled from the small building to the left. The dominating structure of the dock is, of course, The Tower Hotel but if you look to your left you will see the black weatherboarding of a building evocative of the riverside before the docks were built. This building is the *Dickens Inn* and it has an interesting history.

Around 1740 a timber structure was erected near the riverside to house a brewery. As time went by this was turned into a sugar crushing mill and the original construction was covered by a larger building. Only when the dock was being renovated was the old framework revealed and, rather than pull it down, it was decided to make it the core of a new pub. So a new basement was built and the 400 tons of wood were carefully pulled to sit on top. This act of imagination has paid great dividends for huge amounts of beer are once more flowing in the timbered rooms.

Walk towards the *Dickens Inn* along the side of the Central Basin and you will come to a bridge which spans the entrance to the East Dock. This is modern and you will note that both sections of it may be withdrawn into recesses in the dock side. A nifty idea but not new. In fact the original bridge here worked on the same principle and, if you cross the new bridge and walk on for a few yards, you will see the old bridge on display close by a red telephone box.

Time to leave St Katharine Dock now so walk a few more steps along the dockside until you come to the red telephone box. Turn left here and then walk down between two buildings on to Mews Street. Turn right there and then left when you reach St Katharine's Way. Now walk along for a hundred yards or so and you will see Summit House on your right. Just past that is a signpost which indicates a riverside walkway. Follow the path indicated and you will come to an excellent place from which to view that masterpiece of Victorian engineering, Tower Bridge.

Opposite the walkway is Butlers Wharf which is the most densely packed group of Victorian warehouses in London. It was opened in the 1870s, gave service for a hundred years and has now been converted into an interesting complex with restaurants and shops amongst the offices and apartments and an amusing fountain in its central square. To the left of Butlers Wharf, housed in the large white building, is the Design Museum and just behind that a Tea and Coffee Museum which traces the history of the trade in these two commodities.

Today, the river in east London is quieter than it has been for much of the last few hundred years and most of the passing boats are employed in the tourist trade. For several years, recently, there was a riverbus service which offered a quick and comfortable way to travel through the heart of the capital but, unfortunately, this did not prove to be economic and was withdrawn. I wonder what will happen to the redundant riverbuses themselves - will they follow in the wake of one of the earliest steam boats to carry passengers on the Thames? This, the *King William IV*, was employed on the Tower Pier to

Gravesend run in the 1830s but, like the riverbuses, could not plough its way to profitability. Fortunately for its owners, prospective purchasers from Australia were in town and they bought it and then sold one way tickets to would-be emigrants to pay for the four month journey to a new home in the sun. The ship arrived in Sydney in January 1838 and spent the rest of its life steaming backwards and forwards along the coast of New South Wales.

Continue your walk by following the path. Eventually it turns sharp left and runs along side the old western (Hermitage) entrance to the London Docks and then joins St Katharine's Way again. Now cast a glance across the road at the arched entrance to Stephen and Matilda House. This is currently run as a housing co-op but was constructed by planners of an earlier, more municipally minded, era. The old shield above the arched gateway is that of the London County Council (LCC) which did considerable work in improving the living conditions of ordinary working people in the East End. Eventually, the LCC became the GLC, the Greater London Council. The GLC has now also disappeared though its greatest monument, the Thames Barrier, spans the river a few miles downstream and people who live on London's riverside have good reason to be thankful for the forethought. By March 1995 it had been closed 167 times, saving properties upstream from tidal flooding on 22 occasions. On February 1st 1995, for example, it held back the spring tide and there was a difference of 8 feet between the water levels on each side of the barrier.

Turn right when you leave the riverside walkway and cross towards the single storey building which stands at the junction of Thomas More Street and Wapping High Street.

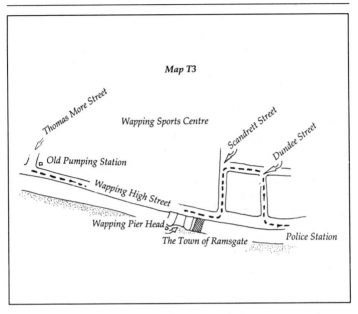

Map T3

Thomas More Street to Wapping Police Station (Map T3)

The building at the junction of Thomas More Street and Wapping High Street now houses a studio but was once a pump house. Note the large metal plaque which indicates ownership by the Port of London Authority, the body originally charged with control of the Thames and its docks all the way from Teddington to the point, seventy miles away, where the lightship you passed in St Katharine Dock once floated. Look also at the gateposts which stand by the side of the old pump house. These date from the construction of the London Docks almost two hundred years ago (the London Docks pre-dated St Katharine Dock by about twenty five years). You might think that their irregular stone caps are just disfigured by weathering but this is not so. They were originally carved this way to suggest dripping patterns of the sea.

Strike out down Wapping High Street passing the *Scots*

Arms on the way. From here you may walk runs down to Canary Wharf through a series of medieval riverside hamlets which at one time were separated by marsh or fields. These natural or agricultural open areas are long gone although there are a couple of small parks by the river and several sections of walkway like the one you have just been along. Look out also for the 'stairs', narrow paths with steps at the end which run down to the river Thames. Getting to the riverside has long been a bone of contention in this area. In medieval times some landowners tried to charge poor people for crossing their land to wash their clothes but the authorities supported those who wanted to do their laundry and put a stop to the attempt to make money out of them. The stairs still allow access to the river and were well used for many years by watermen who operated 'water-taxis' on the Thames.

Wapping is the first of the hamlets. Even before it expanded to serve the needs of the enormous increase in trade in the 19th century it was a busy little community but the coming of the London Docks radically changed the place and little is left from the days before the Napoleonic Wars, let alone earlier.

After following Wapping High Street for a few hundred yards you will come to Wapping Pier Head where, on your right, you will find two rows of houses that date from 1811. They face each other across a patch of grass and you might guess this to be an ancient riverside square. You would be mistaken. These houses were constructed on either side of the main river entrance to London Docks and their sash windows have reflected all kinds of ships in their life.

Hard by the Pier Head stands one of the last remaining pubs of old Wapping. The *Town of Ramsgate*, albeit under another name, was vending ale long before the London Docks were thought of and is associated with, amongst other things, the capture of 'Hanging' Judge Jeffries. Jeffries aquired this nickname as a result of sentences passed on those found guilty of rebelling against King James 11. When James was forced to abdicate in 1688 Jeffries, conscious of his reputation, naturally thought that it might be better to leave the country too and after suppplying himself with adequate funds for his exile (at least

Wapping Bridges

Ship access to the London Docks was through channels. Roads were carried over the channels by moveable bridges. The type of bridge shown below (which you will cross if you do the next walk) was originally powered by pressurised water - as, in fact, were the bascules of Tower Bridge, the lifts of many hotels and the safety curtains of some theatres.

30,000 guineas and plenty of silver) he boarded a collier bound for Hamburg. Had he remained on board until the ship sailed, he would probably have lived out his life with other Stuart emigres in Paris or Rome but he decided to have a last drink at The *Town of Ramsgate*, then known as the *Red Cow*. This was to undo his plans for he was spotted, attacked and had to be rescued from the mob by soldiers. They took him to the Lord Mayor of London (who promptly fainted when he saw who had been brought before him) and Jeffries was taken, evidently at his own request, to the safety of the Tower of London. He died, still only 41 years old, in the following year.

The coming of the docks removed most of the old taverns which gradually fell to the warehouse builders. Now however, the warehouses themselves have experienced a change of use. The one next to The *Town of Ramsgate* was converted into an apartment block some time ago and this type of adaption is currently common not only in London Docklands but also in old canal and dock basins up and down the country.

After walking on past The *Town of Ramsgate* you will come to the junction with Scandrett Street. Turn up Scandrett Street noticing the newly renovated old school building and lantern house on the right. Straight ahead you will see a high wall, one of a decreasing number that remain from the days when they kept thieves from the docks. No dockers sweat behind the bricks today though, just people 'workin' out' at Wapping Sports Centre. Turn right at the corner of Green Bank and cast a glance at the *Turks Head* and admire the tilework. Then look at the freestanding spire of St.John's Church. This and the overgrown ruins are all that remain of a delightful building that dates from the 1760s. It is a pity that the song *Amazing Grace* is not in copyright. John Newton, who wrote it, was born in Wapping and became master of a slaving ship. But he saw the light and took up cudgels on behalf of those poor people being so cruelly transported to the Americas. No doubt he visited his home ground in his middle years and saw this tower when new and I am sure he would have been glad to think that his posthumous royalties would someday be used to repair the sad old fabric.

Proceeding down Green Bank will take you past the solid St. Patrick's Church, a mark of how strong the Roman Catholic influence still is in the area. Beyond the church, turn right into Dundee Street and spy what seems to be a giant block of polystyrene at the end. This is the boathouse of the river police and it is a pity that it is so out of keeping with its surroundings since the association of Wapping and this branch of the constabulary is a long one. The actual police station, the base of the Thames Division of the Metropolitan Police, is a few yards

Scandrett Street - before renovation

down the High Street and you should turn left at the bottom of
Dundee Street to get there.

Wapping, circa 1870

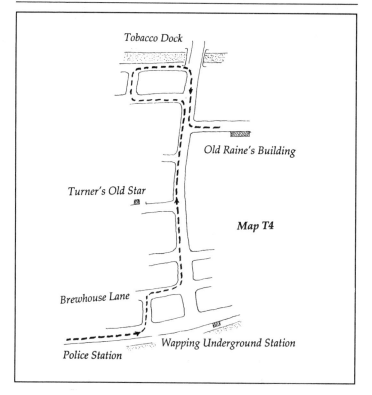

Wapping Police Station to the Old Raine's Building (Map T4)

A force to stop the stealing of cargo was formed in 1798 and was known as the Marine Police. It was the first uniformed police force of its kind in the world and had a difficult and often dangerous job. Equipped with small rowing galleys, the 'Surveyor' and his constables attempted to forestall and intercept raids on merchant ships waiting to unload. Sometimes the result was a frantic night time melee ending in gunfire but the persistence of the law enforcement officers paid great dividends and theft from shipping dropped dramatically. The Marine

Police were amalgamated into the Metropolitan Police in 1839 but the base of river operations has remained at Wapping ever since.

Walking on down the High Street will take you past a pub, the *Captain Kidd* (named after a pirate who was publicly executed in Wapping in 1701) and bring you to King Henry's Stairs. Almost opposite is Brewhouse Lane down which you should walk to see a large, recently renovated block of flats.

Nineteenth-century Wapping, in common with other areas of the East End, had more than its fair share of 'rookeries', small mazes of squalid streets with damp and ill repaired cottages without even the basic amenities. To social reformers, businessmen and small builders these provided a challenge and each group sought to offer something better. Whereas the under capitalised local builder might try to construct superior terraces, it was the block of flats that found favour with the larger interests and the philanthropists. Charles Dickens, whose commitment to social reform was stronger than most, made his position clear;

'It is not desirable to encourage any small carpenter or builder who has a few pounds to invest, to run up small dwelling houses. If they had been discouraged long ago, London would have been an immeasurably healthier place.'

More commercially minded men saw in the flats a profitable investment and, in mid and late Victorian England, many blocks similar to the one in Brewhouse Lane were constructed. When originally let it probably had a waiting list even though the tenants were governed by strict rules. Until the refurbishment a short time ago, something of Dickens' England still hung about the building and it was easy to imagine the soft glow of gas lamps, with each chimney pot smoking, as fuel, carted up the narrow spiral staircases by straining coalmen, began to blaze.

Turn right by the flats past the entrance of the Wapping Campus of the University of Greenwich and walk to Wapping Lane which, rather than the High Street, is the centre of local community life. Turn left.

Our route now runs past the shops and places of refreshment

to the little green at the corner of Watts Street. Stop here for a moment and look left and there you will see the facade of Turner's *Old Star*. The Turner referred to in this case is not a brewer or landlord but Joseph Mallord William Turner who had strong associations with the place. He came east to paint and set up a lady friend as landlady here. One of his greatest works does, of course, have a link with the waters off Wapping. The *Fighting Temeraire* is shown being tugged to its final berth by a clanking little paddle boat. That berth was at Rotherhithe, just across the Thames. What the master of the pallet would have made of the new forms of representation that came after his death I do not know but, iconoclast that he was, I am sure that his ghost will look kindly at the great posters that stand in Wapping Lane. These are usually put up by local action groups who often display their concern about some of the

changes that are taking place in the area.

Continue along Wapping Lane and you will pass the unusual entrance to St. Peter's Church. Note the plaque on the wall to Lincoln Wainright who was vicar here for 45 years. The inside of the church shows it has remained true to the ideals of an earlier incumbent, Charles Lowder. Lowder, who is remembered in the name of the block of flats opposite, was a charismatic, almost saintly man much loved by many Wapping parishioners of a century ago.

A little further up the incline you will come to the junction with Reardon Street. Turn left here and walk down until you come to steps leading off to the right. Climb the steps and you will suddenly be presented with two fine old sailing ships (replicas actually) that stand 'dry docked' outside Tobacco Dock.

Tobacco Dock lies at the centre of the old London Docks complex and it would once have been possible to go by water from here to the River Thames through the Hermitage and Wapping Pier Head locks. Another entrance was at Shadwell Pier Head, which you will pass if you do the next walk. The designer of the original docks was Daniel Alexander (who was also responsible for planning a number of lighthouses and Dartmoor Prison) but the noted civil engineer, John Rennie, had a good deal to do with its actual construction.

Today, Tobacco Dock has been turned into a shopping centre and it has a couple of places where you may buy refreshment if you fancy a break or if you just want to have a good look at the construction of the old wine vaults. If you go right to the other side of the building you will get a good view of St George in the East, a church designed by Nicholas Hawksmoor.

Having reached Tobacco Dock this walk comes to an end. If you want to get back on to the Underground system or walk on to Canary Wharf turn right and walk to the arch which allows access to Wapping Lane. On Wapping Lane turn right and walk down to the junction of Raine Street which is on the left. Those going to the Underground should continue straight down Wapping Lane to the junction with Wapping High Street where they will find Wapping Station. Those walking on to Canary Wharf should walk down Raine Street to the redbrick building which is the old Raine's School dating from 1719. This was originally built by Henry Raine, a man who made money from brewing at the turn of the 18th century. The school was known locally as the 'Hundred Pound School' since, twice a year, a lottery was held for ex-Raine's girls who were to be married. The prize was 100 gold sovereigns, a fortune in those days. The tradition has, unfortunately, long died out though the old lottery can survives as does Raine's Foundation School itself which now has a home in Bethnal Green and celebrated its 275th birthday in 1994.

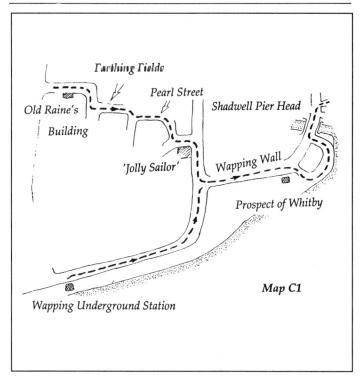

Map C1

Wapping Underground Station

The Old Raine's Building to Shadwell Pier Head (Map C1)
Continue down Raine Street and follow it round to the right.
Immediately you will see a road leading off to the left called
Farthing Fields. Walk down here then cross Penang Street and
walk along Pearl Street which is almost opposite. Follow Pearl
Street round to the right and you will come to the junction with
Prussom Street. Turn left here and walk along past the *Jolly
Sailor* and then turn right down Garnet Street. This will take
you to the junction with Wapping Wall where you must turn
left.

Now read on from the second paragraph of page 66.

The Wapping to Canary Wharf Walk

Introduction

This walk runs from Wapping Underground Station to the Docklands Light Railway Station at Canary Wharf. It should take about 2 hours.

By the middle of the 19th century the riverside villages which had stood on the north bank of the Thames between the Tower of London and the Isle of Dogs had been developed to such an extent that it was hard to see where one one ended and another began. On the waterside, and in the docks which stood behind them, there was constant activity as dock workers went about earning their living in physical conditions which were often very tough.

This walk runs from Wapping, where some of the warehouses are still in use as apartments, down to the site of the old West India Docks, which has now been now redeveloped under the supervision of the London Docklands Development Corporation. Although the docks and their workers have been gone for some thirty years (and huge changes have taken place in the area in that time) there are still many reminders of the days when this area of London was part of one of the greatest ports in the world. Also, occasionally, there are buildings which date from the days before the Industrial Revolution when a road journey from, say, London to Limehouse would take a visitor past orchards and flocks of grazing sheep.

Wapping Underground Station to Shadwell Pier Head (see map on page 64)

Leave Wapping Underground Station and turn right into Wapping High Street. Walk along for about three hundred yards and, after the road bends left, you will see Wapping Wall leading off to the right. You should walk down there.

Walkers from page 64 join here.

Walking along Wapping Wall you will pass warehouses which seem to have a good deal of their original 'business furniture' still intact. It almost seems as though this is a bit of 'bet hedging', like on one of those Viking churches which had pagan symbols carved on the woodwork so that if new ideas did not quite work out, a quick conversion could be made back to old usage.

Wapping Wall, which takes its name from a bank, several feet high, that once acted as a defence against the Thames, leads on imperceptibly to the old riverside hamlet of Shadwell. Beyond the warehouse you will come to one of the best known pubs in the country, the *Prospect of Whitby*. This dates back to the early 16th century and was once known as the *Devil's Tavern* - evidently an allusion to the character of many of the clientele it once attracted. A change in name came about in the late 18th century, the new name being taken from a ship that was moored nearby. Opposite the *Prospect of Whitby* is the ivy covered tower of the old Shadwell Pumping Station which was once used to pump water through a network of iron pipes to many parts of London. Beyond the *Prospect,* turn immediately right along the indicated riverside walkway and you will suddenly have a vista of the Thames before you. After you have followed the path along the riverside you will come to another old entrance to the London Docks and you should follow the walkway around to the bridge which crosses the channel. Then bear right and cross the bridge.

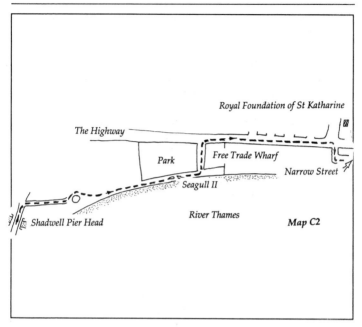

Royal Foundation of St Katharine

The Highway

Park

Free Trade Wharf

Narrow Street

Seagull II

River Thames

Shadwell Pier Head

Map C2

Shadwell Pier Head to Narrow Street (Map C2)

Once over the bridge and past a brick and concrete shelter, you will see a path leading off to the right which leads to the King Edward VII Park. Walk down the path and you will come to a large circular wall with apertures decorated with the intertwined letters LCC. This structure is an exhaust funnel for the Rotherhithe Tunnel which runs below the river here. Go past the circle by bearing left and you will see a plaque erected to those explorers who once embarked here to try and find a new way to the east via the Arctic. Your destination, although east too, is not nearly so far away and you will get a good view of it as you pass along by the riverside railings. Walking along towards two large, ziggurat shaped blocks of flats will take you towards another invisible border, that between the Shadwell and Radcliffe.

Pass through a gate at the edge of the park and you will see a barge called the *Seagull II* one of the last remaining sailing vessels which carried gunpowder along the Thames. Walking further along the walkway will take you to the point where the second ziggurat abuts a warehouse. This warehouse and the other which stands close by it, are now two centuries old. They were originally built by the East India Company which, at the time of their construction, had the monopoly of trade between Great Britain and India and China. One important import of the company was saltpetre (used for making gunpowder in the Tower of London) and it was this product which led to the construction of these warehouses. In July of 1795 a fire began in the premises of a local barge builder which quickly spread along the riverfront and on to vessels moored nearby. One, unfortunately, was loaded with saltpetre and when it blew up it threw burning fragments far and wide and these set light to East India Company property and much else besides. Opinion at the time held that the Great Fire at Radcliffe may have burnt more houses than any other fire in the capital since the Great Fire of London in 1666 so it was hardly surprising that, when the damage was surveyed, the East India Company determined to build new warehouses that were to be as safe a storage space for their saltpetre as possible.

In the next century the warehouses were acquired by new owners and were renamed Free Trade Wharf in the 1850s. This new name may have been intended as some kind of celebration of the reduction of tariffs that marked the years following the repeal of the Corn Laws, ironic though that it should have been these warehouses, which had been built on the profits of a jealously guarded monopoly, that took that title. A hundred years later, Free Trade Wharf was still thriving though saltpetre had given way to rubber, canned goods and matches but, inevitably, the complex was to go the same way as the rest of this part of docklands and the site was redeveloped.

Now walk away from the river passing between the warehouses and the old LMS rolling stock currently being used as ornamental plant stands. Leave Free Trade Wharf through the gateway which still bears that name and turn right.

Window at Free Trade Wharf

The road along which you will now pass is called the Highway and, as you walk, you will notice that you seem to be approaching what looks like a miniature power station with small green chimneys. When you get very close you will see that the Highway appears to be swallowed up beneath this building for it is not a power station at all but a 'portal', one of three which control the traffic and subterranean environment of the Limehouse Link. The Limehouse Link is an underground road, part of the new infrastructure built to ease congestion in Docklands and the surrounding areas. Construction of the link was not cheap, indeed at approximately £3,611 an inch (£255,000,000 for 1,968 yards) it must be the most expensive road ever built in Britain. On the portal you will notice a whirl of black figures. The Limehouse Link Public Arts Competition was organised to encourage local artists to submit designs for works of art to adorn the portals and the black figures are part of a winning abstract sculpture 'Restless Dream' by Zadock Ben-David.

To the left of the entrance of the Limehouse Link are a set of old fashioned lamps. These stand over the entrance to another tunnel, the Rotherhithe, which allows vehicles and pedestrians to pass to the south bank of the Thames. Beyond the lamps are trees which, in turn, help to shield the house that is now home to the Royal Foundation of St Katharine (see p.48).

Time to leave the Highway now for, as pedestrians are banned from the Limehouse Link and we must go on towards Canary Wharf via Narrow Street. The entrance to Narrow Street lies to the right, close by the point where the main road begins to run down into the tunnel.

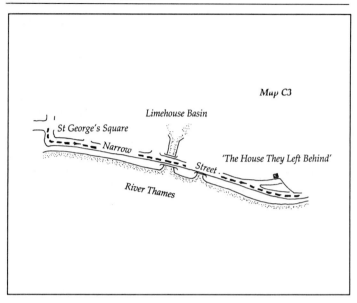

Map C3

Limehouse Basin

St George's Square

Narrow

Street

'The House They Left Behind'

River Thames

Along Narrow Street (Map C3)

Once in Narrow Street follow the road around to the left and you will pass St. George's Square which seems to have something of the medieval about it, even though the date sign says 19, not 13, 87. As you walk on, the rattle of traffic all but disappears and you will find yourself passing more warehouses converted into flats. Narrow Street is the old link between Radcliffe and Limehouse, a place which takes its name from local limekilns where chalk, which had been brought from Kent, was burnt to turn it into a material used in the building trade. Lime burning and other modest scale industries like ship repairing and small tonnage shipbuilding probably had low nuisance factors and so did not frighten away those who wanted to live in an open and healthy place close to London. It was, of course, a very convenient place to live if your work was linked with the sea. At the time that the East India Company was building its

saltpetre warehouses, Limehouse seems to have been a pleasant, almost semi-rural, place. A fine church designed by Nicholas Hawksmoor could be seen for miles, its tower and lantern rising above the roof tops of low rise buildings which were surrounded by 150 acres of land given over to pasture and market gardening. Some buildings which were standing at that time are still there today although Limehouse changed radically in the 19th century.

After walking a couple of hundred yards down Narrow Street, you will come to a bridge which crosses the entrance to Limehouse Basin. Pass on to the middle of the bridge and look around.

To the south the river can be seen and beyond that lies a land which, to many people who spend all of their lives north of the Thames, is (as Neville Chamberlain once said of Czechoslovakia) *'a distant country of which we know little.'* I do not believe I am alone in feeling that the south bank of the Thames is further than it looks, the difficulty of crossing making it a watery psychological divide. In the past, it was easier to cross the river by ferry. Look right and you will see the sign for Horseferry Road, the last reminder of a cross-river route established under an Act of Parliament which gained its royal assent in 1755. Today, like most of the other waterborn traffic, the small horse (and people) ferries are long gone. Maybe if more crossings could be made by tunnel then things would feel different but only a couple are open to pedestrians today. A foot tunnel which was dug from the opposite shore by the Thames Archway Company in 1805 was abandoned even though it had reached a point just below the low water mark on this side of the river. I wonder what remains of that now?

To the left of the bridge is a little corner reminiscent of times when Limehouse Basin was a centre for trade. The reminders of those days are gradually fading away but note the advert, painted on the wall, for a shipping line that provided its own smoky contribution to busier days on the Thames when it sent cargoes to Boulogne, Dunkirk, Calais and Treport by regular sailings. Those cargoes may have been taken to and from the river along the Regents Canal which feeds into the basin that lies behind you. This basin was where the world of the old salt who, maybe, knew Hamburg, Cape Town and San Francisco, blended with that of the bargee whose experience was restricted to Birmingham and Paddington. Each life had its attractions and hardships. I wonder how many youngsters on the barges looked longingly at the tall masts of the old sailing ships passing up and down the river and wished they could be off round the Cape of Good Hope or how many worn out sailors, dreading the roaring forties again, were tempted to spend the rest of their life leading a horse besides the slim blue snake of an English contour canal.

Leave the bridge and continue down Narrow Street and you will soon come to another bridge, this time fixed and seemingly under threat from the wilderness on either side. In front of the decaying cottages buddleia (which, like nature's bailiff, always seems intent on reclaiming the world from man) thrives and, aided by wind and birds, sends out colonising seeds to the surrounding walls. Here, with as much tenacity as a mountain climber, each crevice is sought as a foothold. The bridge itself has been crossed by the plantlife and looking at the river from here may only be done through a leafy border.

A few yards further along Narrow Street, the plants become much more well behaved. Trees and bushes are selected, clipped and docile and the mortar between the bricks so new and smooth that any seed which landed could only tumble to the ground far below. There, even if it did root, it would meet its match in regular maintenance and the hoe.

Beyond Papermill Wharf, you will see that Narrow Street seems to become a wider street and an interesting triangle appears. Don't be put off by the open mouth of the great bird, this is only a model of a seagull (standing on real rope) though I am glad no-one had the idea to match it with a scale model squawk as that would empty the Thames of catchable fish in a few minutes. To the riverside of the seagull is a fine terrace of four storey houses which date from the 18th century and which have survived the Great Fire of Radcliffe, the Blitz and

the attention of demolition contractors who may have set about them in the 1960s given half a chance. Luckily the houses, which were once the home of wealthy merchants, were preserved and found new owners who valued their river frontages and who were willing and able to restore them. To the right of the row of houses is the *The Grapes* a long established pub which may be the one Charles Dickens had in mind when he wrote *Our Mutual Friend* and created *The Six Jolly Fellowship Porters*. Dickens was a regular visitor to the area and his step-father lived round the corner in what is now Newell Street.

In modern times the terrace had its quarter of an hour of fame when David Owen, who had been Foreign Secretary in the Labour Government of the 1970s, made the 'Limehouse Declaration' here. This led to the setting up of a new political party, the SDP.

Leaving the triangle (noting as you do *The House They Left Behind* which, it seems, they did) and pushing on towards Limehouse Causeway you will pass the new park, Ropemakers Walk, on the left. You will also see that you have entered an area of traffic calming. When I first saw the signs for this I had visions of a big hand that would fly out over cars and start to stroke their bonnets as loudspeakers relayed a sympathetic message from some central control unit. I soon found out it meant ramps in the road.

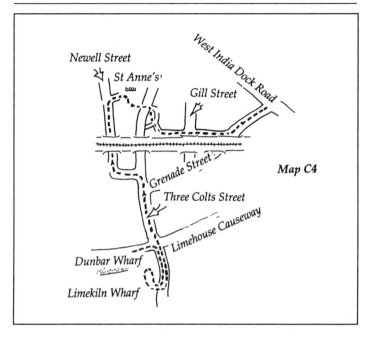

Map C4

End of Narrow Street to West India Dock Road (Map C4)
After a couple of hundred yards you will come to the junction of Three Colts Street, Narrow Street and Limehouse Causeway where you should stop for a moment. By the end of the reign of Queen Victoria, the name Limehouse had become linked in the public mind with something quite different to burnt chalk, shipbuilding or market gardens. The reason for this lay partly with the establishment of a small Chinese community in the area. This seems to have begun with the settlement of sailors who had decided not to take a passage home after arriving as part of a crew of a cargo ship and who began to provide services for other mariners who were just passing through. It was not long before novelists and journalists began to focus on this new aspect of East End life and books like Wilde's *A Picture of Dorian Grey* revealed the supposed secrets of the Limehouse opium

den. In the early 20th century, story tellers like Thomas Burke and Arthur Ward (writing his tales of Dr. Fu Manchu under the nom-de-plume Sax Rohmer) fed the public appetite for exotic happenings 'east of Aldgate Pump'. Indeed, there was a growth in the Limehouse tourist trade, curiosity being given the odd prod by articles penned by travel writers of the status of H.V. Morton. In 1926 the Rector of Limehouse, the Rev. J. R. Powell, irritated by the image given to his parish, wrote that the visitors who came 'slumming' were thrilled *'with the thought that at any moment they may be stabbed in the back or spirited away into an opium den. Every grating distils for them the mysterious odours of some Eastern drug. The vivid imagination of the short story writer enables them to penetrate the secrets of Chinatown to their heart's content.'* But he then went on to point out the overwhelming reality of Limehouse life and what would actually be seen; *'hard working orderly men and women ... and delightful children'.*

Despite the Rev. Powell's objections, the tide of sensation seeking tourists was not stopped and some seemed to make a point of a visit as part of a publicity campaign. For example, Miss Delores Del Rios, a Mexican film star of the silent movie era 'disguised' herself in a plain frock, wool stockings and cloche hat and went down to Limehouse in the company of a *Daily Mail* reporter. She was, she said, looking for 'underworld types' to gain knowledge for a film in which she was to act. Her disguise does not seem to have worked very well, however, the following day saw a complete report of her visit along with a photo of her in a Chinese restaurant. One high spot came when she put her signature in a visitor's book which already contained the names of *'people of the underworld'* and *'world famous celebrities'.*

At the time of Miss Del Rios' visit, Limehouse Causeway was the centre of that part of the Chinese community which had its origins in Canton and southern China. As you can see, nothing is left to remind you of that aspect of life in the earlier part of this century, bombers and planners having long since done their work.

Leave the junction by turning right from the point where

Narrow Street becomes Limehouse Causeway and walk down Three Colts Street. You will go around a slight right hand bend and then come to Limekiln Wharf. This is where some of the original kilns which probably gave their name to Limehouse once stood. To the right, by the side of Limekiln Wharf, you will see a red brick parking area with a low white wall beyond it. Walk to the wall and you will see you are by a creek with the buildings of Dunbar Wharf on the other side.

'The creek beside which the Dunbar Wharf Buildings are built ..... still retains some measure of old world picturesquness' reported one newspaper published in 1923. Seventy years on, the same could still be said and a small drawing of the wharf printed alongside the old article shows a scene recognisably the same as today. The wharf is named after Duncan Dunbar, a man of Scots descent, who built up his own shipping fleet in the mid 19th century. His vessels were beautifully designed and perfectly crafted sailing ships. These visions of grace and swiftness were built of Burmese teak, mostly in the shipyards of Australia. They flew under the company flag and often Dunbar was incorporated in their names so I suppose there were, in ports around the world, ships spotters who really wanted to see every ship with Dunbar in its name. Unfortunately, the fleet seems to have seen more than its fair share of drama on the high seas with tragic results for several vessels. One ship, the *Dunbar*, was heading for Sydney in Australia and began its approach in the wrong place. Evidently a gap in the cliffs had been identified as the harbour mouth and, by the time the mistake had been realised, it was too late. The *Dunbar* was wrecked and all on board, bar one person, were drowned.

Retrace your steps to Limehouse Causeway and cross over onto the northern part of Three Colts Street. Keep on walking for about a hundred yards and you will come to the Cyril Jackson Primary School on the right which sports its own weather vane and impressionistic ceramic map of docklands. Opposite the school, Newell Street runs off to the left and you must follow this street round under the railway bridge. Then you will find yourself in front of another terrace which has somehow managed to survive for a couple of hundred years. As

you walk to the end of it you will come to a lane leading off to the right which runs to St Anne's Church. Go down this lane.

St Anne's Church was built in the early 18th century to the design of Nicholas Hawksmoor, an architect who had mastered his craft with Sir Christopher Wren. The clock you can see is the highest church clock in London and the church tower, a landmark as soon as it was built, must have been a welcome sign of home to many thousands of sailors over the past three centuries.

Bear right as soon as you go through the churchyard gateway and make your way to the south wall on the path. When you reach the wall you will see that the path, here flanked by rows of gravestones, runs out of the church

grounds. Follow the path and then walk over the road to the little triangle of trees and grass that stands close by the old Church Institute, now converted into apartments. Go directly across the triangle, cross the road on the other side and then walk slightly right and go through the entrance to the footpath which runs between the gardens of Joseph Irwin House and the railway viaduct. This will bring you out at Gill Street which you should cross before walking directly ahead on the footpath. Now you will come onto Grenade Street. Turn left on Grenade Street and walk along until you come to the junction at the wide double carriageway of West India Dock Road.

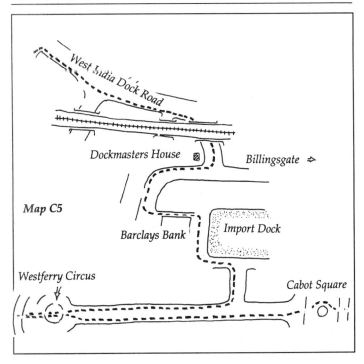

West India Dock Road

Dockmasters House

Billingsgate ⇨

Map C5

Barclays Bank

Import Dock

Westferry Circus

Cabot Square

West India Dock Road to Canary Wharf Tower (Map C5)

Turn right and go down West India Dock Road noting Mandarin Street (evocative in name only) and then cross Westferry Road. If you look left after crossing Westferry Road you will see a row of shops and two friends. The *New Friends* and the *Young Friends* are Chinese restaurants which are a link with the old days of this part of Limehouse Chinatown and stand in an area where people from Shanghai mostly settled. In the 1960s, the original Old Friends restaurant was set up by an ex-cargo ship cook named Lo-Cheong and there have been Chinese restaurants in the area with the name *Friends* in their title ever since.

Continue to follow West India Dock Road and you will come to the junction with Garford Street (which contains some interesting old cottages) and then a railway bridge centrally supported by six pillars. You will see that the old West India Dock Road is blocked off here but you must pass on to the last few yards of it. Go under the bridge to the red-brick herringbone pattern road. Here you will find the fine old Dockmaster's House which, flanked by weeping willows, stands on the right and you should stop there for a moment.

West India Dock Road once led to the West India Docks which were the first of the docks to be completed in the 19th century. As the River Thames makes a great loop to the east of London so it delineates an area of land that, on a map, looks like a drop about to fall. The area is called the Isle of Dogs, a name which has given rise to endless speculation. Despite the fact that it is often referred to as 'The Island' by many residents, the Isle of Dogs has always been a peninsula. In the past, however, it is more than likely that poor drainage sometimes made part of the area seem as though it was as cut off as an island. As for 'Dogs', a commonly held view is that this term originated with Royal Kennels maintained here by a number of monarchs in the medieval period.

Whatever the background to the name the Isle of Dogs was, in the late 18th century, marsh land. Not squashy, soggy salty marsh but pasture marsh, low lying, protected by a bank like the one at Wapping (but here called the Marsh Wall) and home to sheep and windmills. It had a small population but was basically an undeveloped agricultural site in which long holes could be easily dug and filled with river water. Obviously, this was the perfect place for building a dock and William Jessop, an engineer with much experience in canal construction, was engaged to design a complex that would serve the needs of the West India Dock Company.

When opened, the West India Docks were something of a wonder and attracted admiration far and wide. They probably attracted less welcome attention too and, perhaps, some of those who had made a living by stealing from boats and open wharfs made a surreptitious reconnoitre of the dock perimeter to see if they could find a weak point through which to make a foray. If so, they would have been disappointed for not only was there a protective moat but, behind that, a wall topped with railings, too. The only way in, by land, was through the gates, one of which stood between the two piers you can see

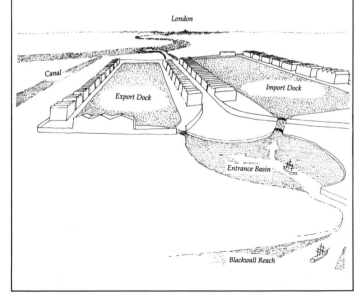

West India Docks

It was anticipated that ships would sail from Blackwall Reach into an entrance basin. From here they would go to either the 30-acre Import Dock or the 24-acre Export Dock. Both docks were to be serviced by secure warehouses. Exit was to be via a basin at the west end. The canal to the south was dug to make a short cut across the Isle of Dogs.

before you. Even if a thief got past these obstacles he would find difficulty in getting close to any cargo by using the windows of the storing rooms and, if you look at the great warehouses that stand behind the piers, you will see why. Nor did the dock owners rely just on bricks and water for security; within the walls the supervision system was well organised and a body of strong men could be relied upon to apprehend those intent on theft.

Turn round now and look back towards the railway bridge. A railway has run over this spot for more than 150 years and the pillars are Victorian originals. When first opened in the 1840s, the line ran between the Minories and Brunswick Dock which is about a mile further east of the bridge. At each of these places a winding engine was built which, by the use of miles of rope, dragged the rolling stock backwards and forwards between them. This may seem very primitive today but such systems were quite common in the early days of railway; stationary engines hauled carriages up the steep incline out of Euston station, for example, and some of those emigrants to Australia who were to join the *King William 1V* in Whitstable (see p 52) may have used the early 'pull-along' line out of Canterbury.

Turn round again and walk past the pillars on to Hertsmere Road. Look left here and you will see Billingsgate Fish Market a couple of hundred yards away. From a distance the market may look as though it is a new structure but, in fact, it is based on an old warehouse once known as Shed 36, North Quay, West India and Millwall Dock. The original Billingsgate was in Lower Thames Street, not far from the Tower of London and market trading may have taken place on that spot for more than a thousand years. Records show that Ethelred the Unready was attempting to enforce customs collection on ships at a place called Blynesgate in 870 and this may have been the Saxon name for Billingsgate. The market was, by law, made purely a fishmarket in 1699 and so it continued for two and a half centuries. Soon after the Second World War however, it became obvious that handling difficulties and traffic problems would probably force a move from the old central London position but it was not until the 1970s that firm proposals were put forward and these led to the establishment of the new market which you can see today. As the merchants and porters (along with their market name) moved to the Isle of Dogs so the old refrigeration units in Lower Thames Street were turned off. Some said that, as the Billingsgate 'perma frost' melted so the old building would probably tumble down but, in fact, it still stands though it looks a little forlorn without its lively trade. For most of the year, the new Billingsgate goes about its business out of the public eye but an annual fish festival is held in the late summer and this is worth going to if only to taste some of the delicious fish dishes on sale.

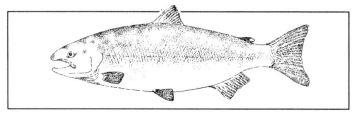

Turn right on Hertsmere Road and begin to walk along and you will pass the Canon Workshops on your right. These were originally built to be used as workshops and offices in the early 19th century. The little round building is about the same age and may once have served as a lock up for those caught in suspicious circumstances - or even red-handed. A short distance beyond the entrance to the Canon Workshops you will see a zebra crossing. Walk over the zebra crossing and then make your way down the left side of the Barclays Bank building. From here you will get a good view of the old Ledger Building which was where the low-tech but meticulous record keeping of the dock trade took place. Clerking here - and there is something very Dickensian about this building which evokes high stools and scratchy pens - was no doubt tedious but such a job gave a measure of security, something the casual labourers who were drawn into the docks on a daily basis never had.

At the rear of the Barclays building turn right and walk along the side of the old Import Dock. Continue along the

walkway round the corner of the dock and then, after a few yards, turn right and walk up the top of the incline. Here you will see an American-style burger bar.

If you have tramped all the way from the Tower of London you may feel fairly whacked by now and be inclined to turn straight left and stagger to Canary Wharf but, if you can manage it, take the opportunity to turn right and walk along West India Avenue to Westferry Circus then cross the road and go to the little park through the decorative swing gate.

This park seems quite mature for its age, a deliberate result of landscaping. Many of the trees planted in this part of Docklands were bought and brought from Germany where they had been growing since the 1950s. Their movement was planned with great care with a maximum of 92 hours being set from the time the trees were lifted to being re-planted. Travelling

by road trailer, mobile woods made stealthy night crossings to Harwich (let's hope no nervous and slightly inebriated person called MacBeth was sailing in the opposite direction!) and were then whisked down the A12 to end their journey close to Canary Wharf in the early morning. Subsequently, as each tree had been carefully identified before it left Germany, it could be put straight into a hole which had a matching number. On a visit to this park in 1994 I was startled to hear an unusual drone overhead and, on looking up, saw a vintage aeroplane. I was even more startled when I recognised it as being an 1930s Junkers and found out later that it belonged to Lufthansa and was on a tour of Britain. Evidently it was on a sightseeing flight over Docklands but my guess is that it was carrying over-anxious German nurserymen making sure that the trees they had raised so lovingly were being properly looked after by their new owners.

Exit from the central island of Westferry Circus by the gate opposite the one you came in on and cross the road. Now go to the railings and you will see a very impressive panorama of London. Looking up river you will be able to identify the places you passed on your way here. Can you see the *Seagull II* and Free Trade Wharf? What about the *The House They Left Behind.* No-one, surely, could miss the tower of St Anne's.

If you could see through time as well as distance this position would be an ideal vantage point too. You could watch the smoke of Boadacea's blaze, the ship which brought Classicianus (see p.46), a boat under the command of a captain who was sniggering because he had evaded the customs collectors of Ethelred the Unready and, in 1066, those victorious vessels which brought the Norman conquerors. By Tudor times the boats would be more sophisticated and you would see some on their way to find a new way to China. By the 18th century the river could be seen to be getting more and more congested until someone made a hole in the riverbank and swept the queues into the docks. Almost at the same time peculiar puffing boats would be on the water too and one would go off to Gravesend one day and never come back. Could you guess where it went?

If you turn and look back across Westferry Circus you will see Canary Wharf itself which never seems quite as tall close up as it does from a few miles away. The 50 storey tower is basically a huge steel frame covered in panels. Before it began to rise, 222 piles were driven 65 feet into the ground and then covered by a 14 foot raft of concrete. A huge amount of building material needed for the construction had to be carefully timed to arrive on site when it was needed and this was facilitated by a computerised delivery system which monitored delivery from a holding base in Tilbury. Naturally, 'Old Father Thames' was pressed into service for the work, much as it had been exactly 900 years before when the ships coming up the Thames were bringing material for the White Tower. There were substantial differences in the scale of work and type of material used, of course. Canary Wharf consumed 30,000 tons of steel in 18,000 pieces which were held together by some half a million bolts whilst the sailing boats employed by William the Conqueror mainly brought stone from Kent, Caen and the Isle of Wight.

All that remains now is to find your way to the Docklands Light Railway Station which stands behind the tower. Retrace your steps, walk along West India Avenue and pass the burger bar. At the other end of West India Avenue you should cross to the central area of Cabot Square where you will find a pool which sometimes turns into a fountain. From here you will see, to the south, the waters of the old Export Dock.

Go to the tower now and pass through the ground floor doors you will see straight ahead. The station is reached by walking through those doors and another pair beyond.

Breathing Space.

(Don't take it for granted)

We don't. Help us keep Britain's breathing spaces open. Footpaths and coastline, high places, heaths and woodland. For walkers.

For 60 years, THE RAMBLERS' lobbying and vigilance have been achieving wide-ranging rights of access to some of our most beautiful countryside.

Go for a walk. Take a breather from our crowded world. Think about the future; invest in THE RAMBLERS.

Join us.

A modest subscription brings you – FREE – the essential Yearbook, full of outdoor information (almost 300 pages, over 2300 places to stay, £4.99 in bookshops), the quarterly magazine, Rambling Today, and membership of one of our 380 local groups. Many outdoor equipment shops offer discounts.

To join, please send a cheque (specifying the membership type you require) to The Ramblers, 1-5 Wandsworth Road, London SW8 2XX. Tel: 071 582 6878

The rates below are valid until 30 September 1996.

Ordinary £16   Reduced* £8   Family/joint £20   Joint reduced* £10

*Under 18, students, retired, disabled or unwaged

60 years working for walkers

Registered Charity No. 306089